SUN DANCERS

DEVI BALA

notionpress
.com

INDIA · SINGAPORE · MALAYSIA

ISBN 979-8-89415-287-5

To

All those who have tasted Love

CONTENTS

AUTHOR'S PEN

VII

History speaks of human achievements and celebrates love as the best of such feats.

When love blossoms the biosphere blooms. When love speaks the universe listens. When love dies the rest of life dies.

It's a pleasure speaking about a few lovers of how they lived and what they gained from such sensational love. Welcome to their lovable world!

ACKNOWLEDGEMENTS

IX

My Eternal Patron

&

All my loved ones

FOREWORD

Dr. Roopkumar Balasingh

Former Head, English, Professor Emeritus (UGC)

Bishop Heber College, Tiruchirappalli, Tamil Nadu, India.

There are people who appreciate prose and there are people who appreciate poetry; it is all a question of acquired taste, or activated delight. None is better or worse than the other since without thought there is no language and without language, we cannot think; it is this very complementation of "reason" and "feeling" that has voted the progress of the new millennial poetry as it has done in this collection of six like the beads on a rosary; and, quite contrastively is no less fiery and feisty in intent in the significance of its titling, Sun Dancers, presenting the "dance of life" in all its paradoxes, ironies and ambivalences.

The poems in "Sun Dancers" reflect on the manifestations of woman or "persona" as Shakthi presenting insights into the very core of creative tension and the resulting quest for relative balance or equilibrium.

Though seemingly less in number for an anthology, the six poems are power packed bespeaking the power of love, life, immortality and most touchingly the quest for the power of freedom to choose, drawn from instances in the Ithikasas like The Mahabharata, The Ramayana, and the Puranas: intangible truths in life are made palpable; the distant divine is made human and tangible; and most importantly the role of woman as Shakthi, the creative power behind creation, life and destruction, who despite her Power is still the benign and benevolent mother and the central balance of all powers whose "third eye glows still, / But drenched in love," making Sun Dancers "poems of power, of love and rebirth"; the ambivalence of fiery destructive heat that is life giving too.

The felt expression of feeling and emotion sans persona; the reinforcement of a much-forgotten fact that the true Centre remains stoically static in its ultimate act of dynamic creation, the spirit of the omniscient, Akhilandeshwari – the Shakthi behind all shakthis - remains Woman.

Sun Dancers offers both, the creative delight of reading poetry and the communicative efficacy of worthy of literary didactics. I am delighted and honoured in presenting a foreword to this collection of well thought out and well executed poems by Dr. P. Bala Shanmuga Devi and I congratulate her for her creative effort.

1. ANTONIUS AND THE NILE

(ANTONY AND CLEOPATRA)

Macedonian her roots

Her charms curled around Rome.

Caesar's pet she was

Antony then, she scored!

Her siblings she saw off

To their abode above.

A brother dipped within the Nile

The next drowned in blood.

Arsinoe her sister,

Escaped her neither!

"Debauched temptress is she!"

Rome called her so.

Replied she in a dozen tongue

No woman to match her

No man either!

Power, she grabbed

Power packed men too.

Held them straight

In the crevices of her arms.

Teamed up the amorous queen

With murder and plot.

A goddess she believed

That she herself was!

A temptress adept

In every stagecraft,

Wrapped in a carpet

Or perched on a barge,

Winner forever, she ruled

By the banks of the Nile

With every way so vile.

Her pompous kingdom

She built and reigned,

For her sons she claimed

Her soil's every grain!

Witch or whatever,

Always a great mother.

Even in Rome,

Her presence turned every stone.

Paraded her love-child Caesarion

Through the hearts

Of every Roman.

Men raised not a voice;

Women admired her poise

Silks and pearls,

Calmed down rumbled noise.

Doting Caesar put her 'stony self'

In the temple of Venus

The erotic 'Isis' gave no choice!

69 BCE was she born

Yet lives anon

The amorous queen on and on.

Debates everywhere go,

To judge and scorn

The ridge of her nose

Or the line of her lips.

Come what may

She claimed the toast

With the slide of her hips.

Her kingdom's safety

Ensured she,

The Macedonian Greek empress.

Egypt was safe

In the curls of her kohl.

A man might rule

With an iron hand

Might kill and make plans...

A woman does the same

But a billion questions

Asks every clan!

Burnt almonds nor

Donkey's milk nor

Cherry red ochre

Became power plants.

Her steal soul and

Her razor mind only

Sowed and reaped grants.

Marcus Antonius second-in-command

Only to Julius Caesar

Bent to the bow of

Her kohl filled eyebrow.

Great Caesar's co-counsel

Felt consoled

At the lap of the 'Nile.'

A word of his, burnt Rome

Along with Caesar's pyre.

Alas, a word from her

Sent Antony to *his* own pyre.

Good to be

One's first love.

Best to be one's last!

Antony and Cleopatra

Held each other steadfast!

Battles he handled cool

In her love he burnt hot.

Roman laws of marriage

He buried in her breasts.

Political giant of Rome

Chose her as his home.

Their twins he loved

Along with Caesar's son.

Rome's pride and,

Caesar's friend

Enemies' terror

A 'man' among men

Melted in the land of *Misr*

The dark soil and the lady,

Laid his sunny soul in

Labyrinthine abyss forlorn.

Enobarbus wondered

How did great Antony miss!

Lo! To receive suicide's kiss.

Kemet, the Black Land

Tells the dark story

For ages since.

How he loved…

How he lived…

How he cried…

Tells not the dark Nile

Why their queen

Let him Die!

Yet tale of their love lives

The greatest of Romans still rules!

Rome's great pride!

Cleopatra's last Love!

The icon of true love,

Even today Antony scores high!

2. VALLI'S VELAVAN

(LORD MURUGA AND HIS DIVINE CONSORT VALLI)

VelAvan:

My twelve eyes condensed within two

I paused and peered at the damsel dazed!

Her hilly fragrance seeping soft

Catapult in hand guarding her corn.

She, taken aback and wondering still

"When will this huntsman be gone?"

She has waited through births

Knowing not when I would come!

Twelve monsoons bygone,

Since she has now born

The little girl of the hunters' clan

Sister of princes seven.

Though a princess she is duty bound

Her father Nambirajan

Had bid her to guard the corn!

His boys all he loved, but

Especial she to the Hunter lord!

The princess of the *mullai*

Soon to be my *kurunji*.

The little maiden looked with awe

As I savour to my fill

Her honey laden eyes, spread wide.

Alarmed, trying to scorn but yet

I knew even then,

The sweet maiden of the tribe

Already to me is drawn.

Puzzled at how I stand and gaze

At her tender physique,

Though not lusty am I.

"How dare you?" she fumes

Her maiden mates too, helpless

Along with my lovely lady!

My Valli! Vellavan's Love!

Bound by the cord

Of previous births strong

Acumen in me never wrong.

Adventure I always seek

This little maiden my hidden virility

Outright seems to greet.

Resolved I to capture her, as

She sees me just a gamester!

Soon her divine Lord she will see,

Though now I appear just an intruder.

A non-native of the land

So, I stand lean a chance to lure

This forest nymph.

"Leave immediately

For fear and love of life"

She bids me anon.

I can hunt a hundred

Any given moment

My Valli knows not yet

That none against me stand a chance!

Her father and his men in no time

I can do away and cast afar

To deadly oblivion at a glance.

Yet, she, my pollen laden breeze

Is no longer scared of me

My honey dew is now scared *for* me.

Her father's arrow she afears

Might kill me, as to her it appears!

I her Lord now knows

She has become mine

Eternal occupant of my shrine!

Fair in war and love

My manhood craves earnestly

To possess the *mullai* maid.

My brother Vinayak I require

To home-in the eternal bride.

The Elephant-God steps in for sure

My Valli to me to lure

Glad indeed that blood is thicker

Than anything ever dear!

Soon, she rams into me

Seeing the Elephant,

Not just onto my chest

My entire being she grabs, and

Two dozen hands not enough

To hold the sweetness manifest.

Three worlds I have conquered

Of all, this is the best!

Nested on my chest

Now knows, that her Sire she has met!

The son of Shiv and Shakti

Warrior Lord of heaven and earth

Embraced by the little tribal princess.

She is all that I have sought

Her dew clad love

Drenched me whole

I have come to take her

Yet, she has taken me!

Her clan not happy,

Tooth and nail they oppose.

The Divine combatant that I am

They all have to fall!

Vanquisher of every opponent

Know not they the hunts men

Nonpareil in seven worlds

Expounder of eons

And they all have to fall!

For her kinsmen Valli cries,

I, her champ decides

To retain her smile.

Alive her kin then arise

My benevolence again nonpareil.

My peeress is now merry

As kinsmen taste a vision rare

My *Vishwaroop* they do cognize!

Nambirajan's pet the princess

Now is his deity's consort.

He the hunter king now is

Proud of his little huntress' hunt

Heaven and earth rejoice

Oneness of romance and love!

My bride I lead home

Icha shakthi now embraces

And leads every tribe.

Mullai's maid is now

Kurunji's eternal pride!

I have conquered millions

And I will conquer still

Eternal patron of divine Tamizh

Keeps lisping love to her

To my hearts fill!

3. ARJUN'S SECOND LOVE

(Arjun and Draupadi)

Arjun:

Avid listener I am

I hear with my cells!

Every follicle of hair

As weapons spread

Tests time, and stories tell!

Very less do I sleep

Even my eye's brow ever alert.

My highbrow to last

With sinews I tie,

Every root of my clan.

The Pandavas, I resolved

To guard with Lord Krish

His benediction guides

I tire not as He holds!

Eternal strife I cross

Turbulence in every sphere!

Every time I begin

A novice, I stand.

The bend of a weapon

The hum of the universe

The rind of the fruits

The hints of danger

The sound of tongues

The tread of animals

The cure of herbs

The dance of heavens

The press of time

The panacea of the flesh

Everything I master.

Infinite river of wisdom

I dive and swim.

No "man" to lead

No "man" to guide

Desolate and lost

Stood my brothers and I.

My broad shoulders

Grow stronger to hold

My first love 'Kandivaa'.

We move from worse to worse

Fatherless children we

Tossed from chaos to chaos.

Mother holds us steady,

And binds us forward.

Holding hands and hearts

Our Draupadi at heels.

I bleed as her feet hurt

No man carries a curse worse.

Her lotus fragrance heals

And holds my heart

That beats for her

My 'second' love.

Lighthouse and a powerhouse

'My' Draupadi sails.

I pine for years

Her tresses to caress

Why am I to share

My "lotus fragrance"?

I fume within, more,

As I see her yearn

For my touch and my turn,

To warm her bed

And hold her in my arms,

That otherwise hold only arms.

The scars on me

None ever read

My victories alone are heard!

Draupadi's touch heals

Every wound I hold

Our souls kept locked

In the warmth of wounds.

I wish for a daughter

As fiery as she is.

Destiny seems so very kind

And refused me this plea.

My sons are my pride

But am I strong enough?

To torch a daughter's pyre.

I cried for our sons

I cried for my clan

And loathed I

As Kunti ma held the hand

Of her 'son' Karna

Draped in the blood

Of Pandu's grandsons.

He, Karna knew,

Whom he slaughtered.

I turned my back

To my ma and her 'son'

My tattered soul

Ripped to shreds

Hit by your screams

Laced with Abhimanyu's blood.

You mothered him better

Than the womb that carried him

Subhadra's son you cared

As you saw *me* in him.

Your loved him as he

Was of *my* blood.

Even Krishna, dear fire

Failed to divert destiny

Awaited there a huge mire

Swallowed us whole

Lessons alone left for

Generations after and after.

My prize from Draupad

Won by my bow,

Cowed down with the burden

Of the curse of our father.

You questioned Dharma

When none other dares to.

Only Bheem you honoured

While at your last breath

"Be born the first

In the next birth",

You say.

"I love you brother Bheem."

For being the hope to my "fire"

When I had gone for ever

And sad enough her distress dire.

Forgive me, my lotus

Forgive me, my fire

You stay my triumph

You stay my conquest

Heaven or earth

None my soul holds

It's yours for ever

My only 'fire'.

4. DIMASA PRINCESS

(HIDIMBA AND BHEEM)

Hidamba:

Daughter of the dark *aaranya*

Am I.

The dense creepers cheer

Every other eye.

I see coyotes and midges

But bat not a single sigh.

Daughter of the fauna

Proud and strong stand I.

My heart rejoices at food

Every other flesh we feed upon.

The *aaranya* gives plenty

My brother Hidimb

And I, Hidimba

Partners in crime stood!

We lure anything

Our palate loves to taste

Flesh and blood fresh and warm.

Draped in dark

We write obituaries,

With the limbs of our feed,

Their blood dipped sand

Grows more love for such

Lovely tasty breed.

Kachar kingdom is ours

Me a Dimasa princess.

Hidimb sends me first

Our potential prey

For me to lure.

Maya I am a magician

Can take any form.

Survival of the fittest dear

No shelter from here.

And, one day when I saw him!

As I walked ahead

My brother following suit

The mission he bid me to do

As his eye drooled on

The biggest of the Pandavas.

"Our food awaits",

I told myself and walked forth

My target was the one awake.

Four men asleep

And an old woman royal

In the folds of my *aaranya*,

Asleep after a burdensome day.

Bheem looked 'delicious' as I

Walked forth as a dusky dame

My magic induced beauty

Camouflaging my asura form.

"No man can resist me",

"Not this one also!"

I said and held my head high

All my assets I flaunted

And walked close by!

Hidimb has bid me clear

"Bring him to me,

We shall drink his blood dear!"

Mighty Bheema looked up

The ravishing beauty he saw

And stood up.

He was to be our prey

But Lord! I was now being eaten!

Besotted I stood a fool.

Captivated was I completely

His eye bore into and saw "me"

The warrior Bheem I saw

Guardsman of his sleeping kith.

I stood frozen and melted low

He neither touched nor spoke

But tore me apart!

I knew I stood no chance

To live as his spouse

We were worlds apart.

Yet I craved for a part of him

Though he stood unmoved.

Pity me dear heavens!

A woman's love is strange.

Pleasure pleases man

Women need more.

My womb woke up to eternity

The urge for motherhood

Screaming to be fulfilled.

I stood a buffer

Between Bheem and my brother

I craved for fulfilment.

Mother of Bheem came to rescue

Bid her son askew

To stay for a year

And give me my heir.

I care not what they schemed.

Strange again, is a woman's love!

Stayed not for long, Bheem

Respected he just my whim

Gave me a son that I deemed

The best of my dreams!

Three sixty-five days hardly

Yet my soul stays happy!

Kachar's girl might never be

Indraprastha's queen and

Bheem left for ever...

I live forever with Katothkach

And of course, my own dreams!

Strange indeed is

The way women love,

And I the Dimasa princess

Not an exception

Though otherwise an enchantress!

Scriptures speak of love found

And also, of love lost.

Better to have loved and lost

Rather never to have loved!

Pity for Draupadi

I stand the first daughter-in-law

Hidden though in the dark roots

Of the *aaranya*.

Hell with the rules of the rich

I stay in heavenly *aaranya*

With my mighty Katothkacha!

5. RUDRA RAAVAN

(Raavan and Vedavathi)

Raavan:

I chant the holy mantra

Invoking the mighty Rudra.

My obeisance only to him

For no human I would hymn.

Rishi Vishrava's precocious child

My father's pride though not I.

With him my first melee.

My fearsome intellect

Makes him so wild.

Forgive nor forget do I.

Born to win, I believe in

Every other scheme I do spin.

I see not the beauty around,

My eyes pierce and rip

Facades and fascists,

Their dirty souls hidden

Behind silk and even saffron.

I spare none.

Every limb I choose to rip,

Every wrong I tear apart.

If adharma prevails,

It must be me that perpetrates

And persecutes.

Foes and friends

I have none.

Foes I wipe off

Fibrils spare I none.

Friends exist not either,

In this badgered land

Of crime and crooked band.

Kumbakarn the only exception!

Parents I love not,

Failures they stand.

Detest I dereliction

Life is but to win.

A very bad boy I am!

When sinews I break,

I blink not an eye.

My cells rejoice,

As I hear a helpless cry.

Dharma or otherwise,

I and only I set the rules,

And break them too.

Taxing rulers' treasury,

Is mine, when I choose.

What was taken, I take away,

Monarchs I crush and

Worms like, they squirm

Under the stink

Of their gore.

Affray I resort not,

My toes suffice.

Fray I, all alone,

My antlers sharpened anon.

When I watch marrows drain

From every bone I break,

My steps falter never.

Yonder when I was five

Vedavathi the Kanyakumari

Landed from nowhere!

I had to suspend tussles

And weapons chilled somewhere.

The lady ascetic nailed me.

Never a word coheres,

As hers!

Never a hope proliferates,

As hers!

In abundance I stood then.

In her limpid eyes

The hiatus in my heart, fills.

Debris of my past rancor laden,

The *Kanyakumari* clears.

A frayed diamond she saw in me

Buried under the detritus.

She picks to luminate

And to animate!

I was about to grow to slit throats

Feeling no flinch of guilt.

She saw that through me,

Astute she grips in a glance.

For once I urge,

Myself to be sapient.

"At least try", she says

"To be good"

I can never try

Yet I do trust her.

My broken diamond crumbs

Feeding upon her.

I freeze as she leaves,

Benumb stands a five-year-old.

I grow into manhood

Hovering upon this "baby love."

I see her bloom into puberty

In filaments of my dreams

My puppy-lady-love

Fills out into a woman,

In the alleys of my dreams.

Her braid's curl and,

The glint of her nose pin,

The cleave of her footprints

I paint in my chamber,

And hold her in my dreams.

I sieve through streets

And search through states

Knowing not where

My lady love now is living.

When then I see her,

She is another man's gain!

Her goodness again

To mighty Raavan, a strain.

All the worlds three,

Helpless I watch

Wondering whence to flee!

My hand and heart itching

To carry her henceforth.

But, she my Vedavathi

Infuses goodwill thenceforth.

I bask in her presence

Engulfed in ethereal love.

Sitting in silence

Perturbed in patience

The only one on earth,

To make Raavan wait!

I wait just happy

To have seen her.

Happy, to have atleast seen her!

I wait in love

Basking at her being,

I wait in love

Knowing not how to fight!

Mighty king Raavan

Waits upon a woman

Ever so in love!

Vedavathi's smile matters

And so,

I wait in love!

Raavan the fighter

Sits seeing her womb swell

Task so cruel yet, I wait

For my only love.

Fate is a gamer to fear

As adharma's follicles

Curl casually around her.

Nooses it, my Vedavathi

And also, her shoots.

A stray thief

A mundane murderer

Knew not who she was!

Petty money he sees

And strangles her through

The child she delivered

To the deep woods

He took and threw.

Raavan's love left for ever

To return here never.

I butcher the thief

Ripping his flesh to rags.

In every sinew I snap,

My diamonds broke to shreds.

My goodness again

I loose

And, stand forever

Desolate and darker still!

The little baby also

I mourn for.

The animal could have spared

My Vedavati's little girl.

Seven heavens I explore

Still searching my soul

Years later I see dawn,

Veda's girl grown and known.

Ram's love Seetha now is,

My Veda's little lass!

In the forest she stays

Tossed in Ram's curse

I can't let it be

Aaranya is not *MY* girl's place.

My fatherly blood

Now distraught,

Scooping her by air

To my palace I bring.

And again,

A curse I wring.

Ram's wife, my girl

Belongs not to a father.

She knows not me

My Veda's little daughter!

Curse befalls Lanka

But, I can't care less.

When, I last bleed to death…

The ticket to heaven's huge abode

I receive with love,

From my Vedavathi's little lass!

6. DEV TO MAHADEV

(Lord Shiva and His Divine Consort Parvathi)

Mahadev:

My tribe I carry

On frozen shoulders

My feet cold,

But never my heart!

The heat of passion

To lead and guard

Leads me far and wide.

Nothing stops me

In spite of every odd.

I lead myself

My conviction alone within!

In my endeavours I stand

Stern and steady

Moving forward,

With sleepless eyelids.

My path I pave

With bare hands

Broken skins and trust

I suffer from,

But never let go my stance!

I move with foresight

Then and ever.

My goals set, to

See everyone prosper.

Rugged my fellow men

Neither royal nor rich

Their lowly life

I resolve to enrich!

Every broil burns deep

It's not for me to ashen.

I wear skulls

Of the arrogant,

My third eye burns

To ashes every demon.

I let not poison permeate,

Pocketed it in my throat!

My men stay safe

And I, ever their Lord!

With the tap of my feet,

I lead and love.

My cosmic dance

Holds all in a swirl.

My voice booms as

Rhythm of the cosmos

Stronger than all.

My tribe knows

That my larynx holds

The key to all doors!

Ethereal and effervescent!

I am loved!

I am colossal!

I am the three worlds!

Experiences of births

Unmatched and unscathed

Only I can propose!

Bound only by duty

Hardly lured by pleasure,

Until I saw *Shakti* I stood!

From the deepest crevice

Of all my three eyes

For once I felt,

The need for another eye!

My journey for ages

From season to season

Weathered and seasoned

My soul's longings

Opened as fountains

As I saw her!

No man I have permitted

To hold my reins

My fury and fire

Known to the entire race.

I stand tall, and all

Stand in awe.

But I give myself to her

Holding her hands,

She awakens and

Puts to ease,

My deepest of pleasures

And the darkest of fears.

How did my red-red eyes

Turn as cool as ice?

She reigns so strong

My lovely Sati

Wraps up my unrest

She casts away all distrust

And every philosophy

Every pulse of eons

That knows not peace,

Now basks in her

My pleasure trove

Filled with ease.

The eternal Shakti

Now resides

Within me as,

My ethereal love!

None other can bind,

A constructive force as I.

I move from palaces to plains

No bond holds me long.

My vision alone drives

My Shakti stands a surprise.

I hold her as my half

Traverses she with me

With will, for eons.

Every cell of mine she shares

And in toto she cares.

Mends and tends

Lends herself with flair

My cosmic dance

Now has a pair!

My third eye glows still,

But drenched in love

To my heart's fill.

Know not I, when

Know not I, how

Know not I, where

My Shakti engulfed

This cosmic dancer whole!

The lady-river on my head

I respect her ever.

She the Ganges flows down

To nourish and care!

But Shakti takes me high

Rules my heart and

The eternal dance we spin.

Erotic or exotic love

My Shakti satiates.

Me, the one

Who feeds entirety,

Hungry and thirsty

For Shakti, I ever be!

In her, my music

In her, my dance

In her, my being

Rests with ease, and

Reaches the zenith!

I for once stand in peace!

Care to share?

Send your feedback to

devibala25.oct@gmail.com